C000179098

Black Roses

Black Roses: The Killing of Sophie Lancaster

Simon Armitage

POMONA

A Pomona Book
P-025

Published by Pomona Books 2012
Telephone: 01422 846900
e-mail: admin@pomonauk.co.uk

www.pomonauk.co.uk

1

A CIP catalogue record for this book
is available from the British Library

ISBN 978-1-904590-29-3

Set in Monotype Bembo Book
Typeset by Christian Brett

Printed and bound in England by
CPI Group (UK) Ltd, Croydon, CRO 4YY

In Memory of Sophie Lancaster

Introduction

In the early hours of Saturday 11th August 2007, Sophie Lancaster and Robert Maltby were walking home through Stubbylee Park in Bacup, Lancashire, when they were attacked by a group of local teenagers. Robert survived, but in trying to protect him Sophie received serious injuries to her head and body, and died two weeks later, having never regained consciousness. When it came to court, the appalling details of the case attracted the attention of the national media, the trial judge describing the assault as an act of "feral thuggery," one which "degraded humanity itself." Five young men were given prison sentences for their part in the crime, two of them for life. Although not treated as such at the time, all the evidence suggested that this had been a hate crime, and that the couple were set upon for no reason other than their unconventional appearance.

Black Roses: The Killing of Sophie Lancaster was a radio drama-documentary, written for BBC Radio 4 and first broadcast in March 2011. The programme consisted of an interview with Sophie's mother, Sylvia Lancaster, interwoven with ten poetic monologues written in Sophie's character. I never met Sophie Lancaster but in everyone's recollections, and especially those of her mother, she was a sensitive, inquiring, peaceable, innocent and defenceless young woman, and through these poems I wanted to give her back her voice. The part of Sophie was played by Rachel Austin, and the programme was produced and directed in Manchester by Susan Roberts.

Simon Armitage

For further information,
contact the Sophie Lancaster Foundation
http://www.sophielancasterfoundation.com

Black Roses: The Killing of Sophie Lancaster

(I was slow to get born,
November's child,
wanted nothing more
than to laze in the sling of my mother's womb,
to loaf and lounge
where it was slow,
where it was warm.
So I sat tight
in a curled ball,
cocooned in love,
gloved, adored.
Hazy colours
and watery sounds
came drifting through.

At odds from the start
I was sideways on,
unengaged,
lying in wait
till my mother's birthday
came about,
then I roused and turned
and shouldered out,

into the day,
out of the dark.)

(November's child is
watchful, calm.
The twilight month,
month of the short afternoons,
the low sun
and the vampire moon.
Were those gothic days where I got it all from?
I kept mum.
I bit my tongue –
why use ten words
instead of one?

When you can use none.

Why speak at all
when everyone else is
babbling, gabbling,
rabbiting on?
At six months old
the house was silent,
the silence that dawns
when a toddling daughter
is there

then gone.
I was only upstairs,
reading phrases and words
beyond my years,
with my head in a book
which was upside down,
the wrong way round.)

(To be sometimes remote.
To be sometimes withdrawn.
Was it such a crime
to be growing up
at my own pace,
in my own way,
in my own sweet time?
They were saying then
that I had what they called
an inquiring mind,
learning quickly
to empathise,
standing there at my mother's side,
hearing the language
of human rights,
hearing the rants of her leftie friends,
Bolsheviks and Trotskyites,
so I ditched the comfort of pillows and sheets
and slept one night
in a cardboard box
in sympathy with the down and out,
and bedded down
in a linen drawer,

because sometimes you need
a place to hide,
a hidey-hole,
somewhere to crawl.)

(I didn't do sport.
I didn't do meat.
Don't ask me to wear that dress:
I shan't.
Why ask me to toe the line,
I can't.
I was slight or small
but never petite,
and nobody's fool:
no Barbie doll;
no girlie girl.
I was lean and sharp,
not an ounce of fat
on my thoughts or limbs.
In my difficult teens
I was strange, odd,
– aren't we all –
there was something different down at the core.
Boy bands and pop tarts left me cold;
let's say
that I marched to the beat
of a different drum,
sang another tune,

wandered at will
through the market stalls
humming protest songs ...

I wore studded dog leads
around my wrists,
and was pleased as punch
in the pit, at the gig,
to be singled out
by a shooting star
of saliva from Marilyn Manson's lips.

But for all that stuff
in many ways an old-fashioned soul,
quite at home
in my own front room,
on my own settee.
I read, I wrote,
I painted, I drew.
Where it came from
no one knew,
but it flowed. It flew.)

(I met a boy.
He was one of me, I was one of him,
we were one and the same.
I went towards him
and kissed his face.
He was skin and bone,
he was six foot tall,
he was ghostly pale,
he was poetry, art,
he was quirky, cool,
he was backcombed and pierced,
he was perfectly weird,
we walked through Manchester
hand in hand,
we were both in league
with the colour black,
not knowing exactly
who we were
but both agreed
on what we were not.
We were joined at the hip
in this photograph,
we were all black t-shirt

and snow-white flesh,
we were silhouette.
I slashed my jeans
and unpicked my seams
and smeared my lips
and ripped my fishnets
in honour of him,
sat at the mirror
for hours on end
with banshee make-up
and hurricane hair
till I looked like I'd fallen out of a tree,
till I looked like I'd clambered out of the grave.
It was love.
It was life.)

(It was one small step
across the street
but one giant leap
into bed-sit land,
and very grown up
to be moving in,
to be given the keys,
to lift the latch,
to be playing house,
to be lady and lord
of our very own place,
in our very own space.

We were dreamers, asleep.
We were jobless, skint,
always juggling
and having to stint,
not a cent to our name,
always struggling
to make ends meet,
to eek things out
till the end of the week.
Never enough

to save or spend,
always a case
of make do and mend.
Couldn't afford
a lick of paint,
kitted it out
with sticks of furniture
borrowed and begged,
splashed each wall
with home-made art,
insulated the hall with books.
We were suddenly dish-washers,
bed-makers, fire-lighters, cooks.

To the passer-by
it was hardly The Ritz,
nowhere to shout
or show off about,
just some old, cold
first floor flat
below the moor,
above a shop,
but to us it was home,

palace and penthouse,
fortress and funhouse,
studio, library
all rolled into one.
We could bolt the door
and keep the world out
or watch the world
as it wandered past,
in all its glory, beautifully mad,

all the nightshift workers and daylight shirkers,
the mods and rockers and emos and moshers
and joggers and bikers and slackers and slickers,
all the swimmers and sinkers and grafters and thinkers,
all the fly-posters and bill-stickers,
the goths and the straights and the groovers and ravers,
the movers and shakers, the candlestick makers …
all the pissheads and potheads and veggies and vegans
and coppers and preachers and posties and traders,
the night-hawks and the dawn-treaders,
the speed-freaks and the metal-merchants,
the skrimpers and savers, the beggars and trail-blazers,
all the chancers and mystics and givers and takers,

the skinheads and suedeheads and non-believers,
all the tattooed crusties, all the crested Mohicans,
all the folkies and rappers and ragamuffins
and rastas and clubbers and dubbers and mixers
and suited commuters and duckers and divers
and salesmen and truckers and lollipop ladies
and beatnicks and peacenicks and streetkids and skaters
and hitchers and drivers and runners and riders,
all the rat-racers and the money servants,
all the dancers and deejays,
all the trippers and heavies and slackers and hippies
and hawkers and vendors and takers and lenders
and the dog-walkers and the dawdlers,
all the late starters and the early risers ...

all the human race
in its crazy parade.

I said let them all be.
I said breathe and let breathe.)

(Summer. August.
The people's month.
Easy, effortless,
endless days.

Think of a park
in its perfect form.
The Victorian dream:
the tick and tock
of a tennis ball,
the applause of leaves,
the sleepwalking arc
of a crown green bowl,
the strains of a band,
swings and a slide,
the deck-chair stripes
of a freshly mown lawn,
a Union flag
at ease on its pole,
an ice-cream stand,
geraniums spelling the name of the town,
Friday night lovers
out for a stroll.

Had we only known ...

that this was a place
where shadows waited,
where wolves ran wild,
where alcohol poisoned
the watering hole.
Up ahead,
cigarette tips and mobile phones
glimmered and sparked,
glinted and squawked
in the valleys and peaks
of the skateboard ramps.
Whatever possessed us,
led us on?
Figures materialised out of the black,
till a group

was a gang

was a mob

was a pack.

Late. Dark.
The hours were small,
the minutes lost.
It was there and then

but it's here and now,
real, actual,
won't go away,
keeps happening over and over again:

in no time at all
an alarm bell chimes,
the barometer swings,
the mercury climbs,
the hour-glass flips,
the galaxy tilts,
the universe spins,

the needle swerves violently into the red

in an atmosphere of menace and threat,
in an aftershave of dope and booze
and testosterone and pent-up hate.

Have we said the wrong word?
Have we made the wrong turn?
Have we strayed from the path?
Have we stepped on their patch?

Do they find offence
at the studs in my lips,
or the rings in my ear?
Are they morally outraged by what we wear?

We are kindly creatures, peaceful souls,
but something of our life aggravates theirs,
something in their lives despises ours.

The difference between us is what they can't stand.

So the blows fly in
with that level of fury
which needs to hurt,
that depth of anger
which goes for the face,
which desires to maim,
and when they have finished

knocking the stuffing
out of my man,
kicking his skull
for all they are worth
and I nurse his broken head on my knee,

one turns on me.

Oh God he comes back and turns on me,
a plague of fists or a swarm of feet,
the boot going in again and again.

How he hates my demeanour,
hates my braids,
how he hates my manner,
hates my ways,

doesn't know me from Adam,
not even my name,
but detests every atom
of what I am.

Nothing I scream for can make it end.

He will kick and will kick
and will kick and will kick
till the living daylight
flies away.

On my hands and knees

I crawl

some way

then fall

then curl.

This is pain beyond pain.

I am seeing stars.

I watch planets wheel.

I feel heavens whirl.

I hear sirens wail.)

(I am dead
but alive,
alive but dead,
ghosting somewhere in between,
cushioned and wrapped
in hospital pillows
and hospital sheets,
blanketed
under fluorescent light,

a medusa of drips and tubes and leads
and clotted braids
and tangled beads

and jigsaw shapes
of naked scalp
where clumps of my hair
were kicked clean out.

The police can't believe
this necklace is mine,
too ladylike,
too feminine.

And mum can't see
that somewhere inside
this swollen, bloodshot, abstract mess
is my heart-shaped face,
my swan-like neck;

black roses that bloom
on my arms and legs
are the bitter bruises
of self-defence.

I am traumatised.

I am compromised.

I am deeply distressed.

I am sorely defaced.

And I'm sorry, mum, to make such a fuss,
to be centre-stage.
Sorry to twitch.
Sorry to mumble

and make no sense.
Sorry to sweat.
Sorry to vomit and arch my back.
Sorry you have to see me like this,
purple and blue,
branded and stamped
all around my head
with the logo and tread
of a training shoe.

I can't find my form,
can't breathe on my own,
can't move my mouth
to say what I feel.

I can't help my feet
when they clench into claws,
can't help my legs and arms
when they thrash,
can't help my eyes
when they roll and track.

Can anyone say if I'm coming back?)

(How distant I am.
How far away.
I am not myself.
Am I still of this world?

One day they think
I might even walk
but my legs and feet
are a law to themselves.
One day they hope
I might manage to talk
but my tongue and my brain
are in separate realms,
on different planes,
not even remotely
on speaking terms.

What heart I have
is all over the place.

What mind I have
has a mind of its own.

I am critical, grave,
beginning to fade,
weakening, faint,
now losing hold,
now slipping below.)

(Do I even know
that my man survived,
whose handsome head
I cradled and kissed
while they beat him with names,
while they stoned him with kicks,
whose innocent face
I tried to shield,
whose life I wrapped and held
with my own?

Will he think me cold
or impolite
if I don't respond
when he says goodbye,
if I lie here unmoved
when they wheel him in
in stitches and pins
for a final time,
body broken,
spirit dimmed.

Mother, mum,
don't think me rude
if my eyes don't light up
at my favourite things,
at these new pyjamas,
this toiletry bag,
but I'm losing ground,
I'm slipping back.

When you loosen my clothes,
please don't be fooled
by the hidden tattoos,
and the studs and rings
in intimate folds,

or the woman's body
I've secretly grown,
because under this skin
I'm your helpless daughter all over again,
your little dot,
your baby girl.

As you did then, do again now:

mop my brow as you mopped my brow,
climb in my bed as you climbed in my bed,
lie at my side as you laid at my side,

as you kissed my ear

as you wiped my mouth

as you soothed me to sleep

as you washed me down

as you bathed my breast

as you put me to rest.

Night follows day,
day becomes night.
I am sunken, deep,
elsewhere, vacant,
out of reach.

They have scanned and searched

for vital signs
but I'm
hardly a pulse,
barely a breath,

a trace,

a thread,

a waste,

a past.

The line on the screen goes long and flat.

Pull the curtains around.
Call the angels down.

Now let me go.

Now carry me home.

Now make this known.)

POMONA BOOKS

Pomona is a wholly independent publisher dedicated to bringing before the public the work of prodigiously talented writers. Our books can be purchased on-line at:

www.pomonauk.com

Pomona backlist